COMHAIRLE CHONTAE ÁTHA CLIATH THEAS
SOUTH DUBLIN COUNTY LIBRARIES

SOUTH DUBLIN BOOKSTORE
TO RENEW ANY ITEM TEL: 459 7834

Items should be returned on or before the last date below. Fines, as displayed in the Library, will be charged on overdue items.

D1615376

THE NUMBERED

Other books by Elias Canetti available
from the same publishers

Kafka's Other Trial (criticism)

The Voices of Marrakesh (travel)

THE NUMBERED

a play by
Elias Canetti

translated by Carol Stewart

Marion Boyars
London . New York

Published in Great Britain in 1984 by
MARION BOYARS PUBLISHERS LTD.
18 Brewer Street, London W1R 4AS.

Distributed in Australia by
Wild & Woolley, Glebe, N.S.W

Distributed in New Zealand by
Benton Ross, Auckland

Originally published by Carl Hanser Verlag in 1964 under the title 'Die Befristeten'.

British Library Cataloguing in Pu~~~~~~~~~~

Canetti, Elias
  The numbered.
  I. Title   II. Die Befristeten. *English*
  832'.912   PT2605.A58

ISBN 0-7145-2814-5 Cloth

Printed in Great Britain by Hillman Printers, Frome, Somerset

Characters

Fifty
The Friend
The Keeper of Lockets

One Man
Another Man

Mother, *32*
Boy, *70*
Man, *Professor 46*
Woman, *43*
Grandmother
Grand-daughter
Young Ten
Two Colleagues
The Couple
A Young Woman at the Funeral of her Child
Two Young Men, *28 and 88*
Two Ladies
Chorus of the Unequal
Two Old Women, *93 and 96*

The first production of *The Numbered* was given November 5th, 1956, at the Playhouse Theatre, Oxford. Directed by Mr. Minos Volanakis.

CAST

The Keeper	Sebastian Shaw
Fifty	Frank Windsor
Fifty's Friend	Edgar Wreford
The Professor	James Maxwell
First Colleague	Frederick Bartman
First Lady	Charmain Eyre
Second Lady	Pat Keen

PROLOGUE

A CONVERSATION ABOUT THE OLD DAYS.

ONE MAN   In the old days . . .

ANOTHER MAN   In the old days. Do you believe those fairy tales?

ONE MAN   But they're true. There are documents.

ANOTHER MAN   Have you read them?

ONE MAN   Of course. That's what I'm telling you.

ANOTHER MAN   And what do they say?

ONE MAN   Exactly what I've told you. A man went out of his house to buy cigarettes. "I'll be back directly" he said to his wife. "I shan't be a minute." He went out of the door of his house and started to cross the road because the shop was on the other side. A car came round the corner suddenly and knocked him down. He lay there. Double fracture of the skull.

ANOTHER MAN   And? What then? He was taken to hospital and recovered. He was in hospital two or three weeks.

ONE MAN   No. He was dead.

ANOTHER MAN   Dead. It was his *moment*.

ONE MAN   But no. That's exactly the joke.

ANOTHER MAN   What was his name then?

ONE MAN   Peter Paul.

ANOTHER MAN   But what was his real name?

ONE MAN   Peter Paul.

ANOTHER MAN   So one is always asked to believe, but do you really think that people then managed to live without proper names?

ONE MAN   I tell you they did. They were called by any name and

the name meant precisely nothing.

ANOTHER MAN   So that anyone could simply change names with anyone else?

ONE MAN   Certainly. It didn't matter what anyone was called.

ANOTHER MAN   And the name had nothing to do with the moment?

ONE MAN   Nothing. The moment was not known.

ANOTHER MAN   I don't understand. You're trying to tell me that no one, not one single person, had any idea of the moment at which he would die?

ONE MAN   Precisely. No one.

ANOTHER MAN   Tell me now, seriously. Can you really imagine such a thing?

ONE MAN   I can't, honestly. That's why I find it so interesting.

ANOTHER MAN   But no one could have stood it, such uncertainty, such fear. I shouldn't have had a moment's peace. I should have been able to think of nothing else. How did those people live? One couldn't have taken a step out of one's house – How could people make plans, how could they embark on anything? I think that's terrible.

ONE MAN   It was terrible. I can't imagine it any more than you can.

ANOTHER MAN   But you believe it, you believe that it was like that?

ONE MAN   That's why one reads history.

ANOTHER MAN   Stories you mean. I can believe that there were cannibals.

ONE MAN   And pygmies.

ANOTHER MAN   And giants, witches, mastodons and mammoths. But this is *too* much.

ONE MAN   What can I say to prove it?

ANOTHER MAN   Perhaps I've never really tried to understand it.
It sounds monstrous. It sounds unbelievable.

ONE MAN   All the same, that's how the world went on.

ANOTHER MAN   Perhaps people were much stupider than now.
Dull.

ONE MAN   You mean like animals? They don't think.

ANOTHER MAN   No. Animals hunt and eat and play without
thinking what may happen to them while they're at it.

ONE MAN   There we *have* made a little progress.

ANOTHER MAN   A little? You can't call those others men at all.

ONE MAN   And yet they painted and wrote and made music.
There were philosophers and men of genius.

ANOTHER MAN   It's ridiculous. Any wretched cobbler now is a
better philosopher because he knows what will happen to
him. He knows when he will die. He can apportion his
lifetime. He can plan without fear. He is sure of his allotted
years and he stands as firmly on them as on his two feet.

ONE MAN   I believe that the manifestation of the moment was the
greatest advance in human history.

ANOTHER MAN   They were just savages before. Poor devils.

ONE MAN   Animals.

PART ONE

MOTHER   Seventy, Seventy, where are you?

BOY   You can't catch me, Mother.

MOTHER   I get so out of breath always.

BOY   You like running after me, Mother.

MOTHER   And you like making me run after you, you bad boy. Where have you got to now?

BOY   Up in the tree, ha, ha! You can't catch me!

MOTHER   Come down at once. You'll fall. The branches are rotten.

BOY   Why shouldn't I fall, Mother?

MOTHER   You'll hurt yourself.

BOY   That doesn't matter, Mother. Why shouldn't I hurt myself? Brave boys aren't frightened of hurting themselves.

MOTHER   All right, all right. But something might happen.

BOY   Not to me, though. Not to me. My name is Seventy.

MOTHER   One never knows and it's better to be careful.

BOY   But, Mother, you explained it to me yourself.

MOTHER   What did I explain to you?

BOY   You said that I was called Seventy because I would live to be seventy years old. You said that you were called Thirty-Two because you would have to die when you were thirty-two.

MOTHER   Yes, all right. But you might break your leg.

BOY   Mother, can I ask you something?

MOTHER   Anything you like, little one.

17

BOY   Do you really have to die when you're thirty-two?

MOTHER   Yes, of course, I explained that to you.

BOY   Mother, do you know what I've worked out?

MOTHER   What have you worked out?

BOY   I shall be thirty-eight years older than you.

MOTHER   Thank God for that, little one.

BOY   Mother, how many years more will you go on living?

MOTHER   That's too sad, child. Why do you ask me that?

BOY   But you will go on living a long time still, won't you, Mother?

MOTHER   Not so very long.

BOY   How long, Mother? I want to know how long.

MOTHER   That is a secret, child.

BOY   Does Father know?

MOTHER   No.

BOY   Does Grandpa know?

MOTHER   No.

BOY   Does my teacher know?

MOTHER   No.

BOY   Does nobody know, nobody in the whole world?

MOTHER   Nobody, nobody.

BOY   Oh, Mother, I must know.

MOTHER   I've said it's a secret.

BOY   Oh, Mother, dear, dear Mother, tell me all the same.

MOTHER   Why do you torment me. It wouldn't be any use if you
          did know.

BOY   I must know.

MOTHER   But, why? Just tell me why.

BOY   I'm so frightened, Mother. Everyone says you will die when you are young. I want to know how much longer you'll run after me. I want to love you so terribly. I'm frightened, Mother.

MOTHER   You mustn't be frightened. You'll be a good and clever man. You'll have a wife and several children and a lot of grandchildren. You'll live to be old, Seventy, and when you die, you will already have great-grandchildren.

BOY   But I don't want them. I only want you, Mother. Tell me.

MOTHER   You mustn't be so obstinate, I can't tell you.

BOY   You don't love me.

MOTHER   You know I love you more than anyone.

BOY   Mother, I can't go to sleep unless you tell me.

MOTHER   You are a terrible boy. You've always been to sleep all right so far.

BOY   That's what you think. That's what you think. I pretend to, but, when you go out of the room, I open my eyes and look at the ceiling. I count the dots on it.

MOTHER   What's the point of that? You'd much better sleep.

BOY   But they are the goodnight kisses that you'll still give me. I count them, I count them, every night I count them but they never come to the same. Sometimes there are a great many and sometimes only a few. You know, I never see the same number of dots. I must know how many there are. I shan't ever be able to go to sleep otherwise.

MOTHER   I'll tell you, little one. You'll have more than a hundred goodnight kisses from me still.

BOY   More than a hundred! More than a hundred! Oh, Mother, now I shall be able to go to sleep.

FIFTY. HIS FRIEND.

FIFTY   It is the best age. I don't believe it.

FRIEND   It's proved so, so far.

FIFTY   I don't believe it. In fact, I can disprove it straight away. You say that the moment comes to everyone at the right time. Give me an example.

FRIEND   I need only look at my own family. My father was called Sixty-Three. He was exactly that age when it happened. My Mother is one of the lucky ones. She is still alive.

FIFTY   What is your Mother's name?

FRIEND   Ninety-Six.

FIFTY   She can't be so old, certainly. But that still doesn't mean
. . .

FRIEND   Wait. Wait. I will tell you something. I had a little sister, an enchanting creature. We were all in love with her. She had long hair and wonderful dark eyelashes. She used to open her eyes very slowly, her eyelashes were like silent wings which carried one up into the heights and yet, at the same time, one lay in the shadow at her feet. That was what was so strange.

FIFTY   You speak of her like a lover.

FRIEND   She was a child. I was older than she was. I was not the only one who worshipped her. Everyone who came near her felt that she was something unearthly.

FIFTY   And what became of her?

FRIEND   She is dead now. She died when she was a child.

FIFTY   What was she called?

FRIEND   She was called Twelve.

20

FIFTY   You never told me this.

FRIEND   I never talk about her. I have never got over it.

FRIEND   Did she know everything?

FRIEND   We often wondered about that. It's not easy to keep
         these things secret from a little girl. They're inquisitive and
         listen to grown-up talk.

FIFTY   Yes. They always have that morbid interest in their names.
         All children have. They torment their mothers till they
         explain everything.

FRIEND   But my sister was different. She never asked. Perhaps
         she guessed that the *moment* would come early to her but,
         if she did, she never showed it. She was so calm for a child.
         She never let herself be hurried. She'd be told, "You'll be
         late for school. You must hurry." "I'm all right. I'll be in
         time," she'd say. And she never was late, although she was
         so slow.

FIFTY   That sounds very unusual for a child of her age.

FRIEND   It was. We couldn't understand it. She never quarrelled.
         She never took anything away from another child. She had
         no special likings. She took pleasure in everything she saw
         and she observed it all in her slow, searching way. I think
         now that to observe was her happiness. She *looked* at
         things as other people *love*.

FIFTY   I wish I had seen her.

FRIEND   Oh, it was long ago. More than thirty years.

FIFTY   We didn't know each other then. She must have had a
         serious illness.

FRIEND   Of course. But we won't speak of that now. I don't tell
         you this for pleasure. I told you her name and you know
         that it came then.

FIFTY   I don't doubt your word.

FRIEND   How could you? It would offend me mortally. Could I lie about such a thing?

FIFTY   No, of course not. It is much too serious for that. But I *would* like to ask you one thing.

FRIEND   Yes?

FIFTY   You will be surprised at my ignorance but, till today, I have always refused to know anything precise about these repellent customs.

FRIEND   There's not so much to know as you think.

FIFTY   Wait a minute. I'll astonish you before I've finished. Have you ever known anyone who has confided his age to you?

FRIEND   I don't understand. What do you mean?

FIFTY   I mean what I say. Has anyone ever told you how old he really was?

FRIEND   A living person?

FIFTY   Who else? Someone who was not alive could not exactly tell you.

FRIEND   If I didn't know you so well, I should say that you were mentally defective, a congenital idiot, a hopeless cretin.

FIFTY   That's why I ask you. I have never yet dared ask anyone this question.

FRIEND   And that is why you ask me?

FIFTY   Yes, I trust you. You won't betray me.

FRIEND   Of course not. If I did that, you'd be put under a legal guardian, or in an asylum.

FIFTY   Of course. Of course. Answer my question and don't worry about the asylum for me. I'll ask it again. Has anybody ever confided his age to you?

FRIEND   No, naturally not. No one does that. No one would

imagine that he could do such a thing. The cheapest scoundrel has more self-respect than that.

FIFTY   Good. You know no one who has ever done such a thing. No one says how old he is.

FRIEND   No. No one. But what is all this leading up to?

FIFTY   How does one know that the moment is a fact? Perhaps it's only a superstition.

FRIEND   *(Laughs aloud)* You don't know that? You really don't know what happens directly someone dies? The death must be officially certified. When the responsible official has done that in the presence of witnesses, he opens the sealed locket.

FIFTY   What locket?

FRIEND   The locket that hangs next to your heart. Where have you lived? You have worn it since birth. It is sealed in such a way that no one can open it. Only the Keeper of the Lockets *can* open it.

FIFTY   Do you mean this? (*He pulls a little locket out from under his shirt and holds it up*) Do you mean this little object?

FRIEND   Don't joke about it. Yes, I mean that little object.

FIFTY   I've never known why one had it. I remember that from the time I was small, people nagged me to look after it. My mother took pains to frighten me about it. She said that if I lost it ever, or if anything happened to it, I should starve.

FRIEND   And she was quite right, but for reasons you couldn't understand then.

FIFTY   I thought the whole thing was a fairy tale.

FRIEND   But have you ever tried to open the locket?

FIFTY   No. No more than I've tried to cut out my heart.

FRIEND   You were a virtuous child. It's a good thing that you have

23

remained so virtuous.

FIFTY   And if I had opened it, what should I have found in it?

FRIEND   The exact day of your birth. The exact year of your death.
Otherwise nothing. The locket is hung round the child's
neck immediately after the birth ceremony and is not
touched again until the Keeper of Lockets takes it into his
hands.

FIFTY   And that is sufficient proof?

FRIEND   It *is* proof. For the child, as soon as he can speak and
understand, learns from his mother how old he is. It is
impressed on him under threat of severe punishment that
he must say nothing about it to anyone. Perhaps you don't
remember that?

FIFTY   Yes, yes. I believe I have such a birthday too.

FRIEND   If one finds the same birthday in the locket as the one he
knows, and if he dies on the same day, isn't that proof
enough?

FIFTY   It proves that a man dies on his birthday, but he might do
that out of fear of his birthday . . .?

FRIEND   But he also knows how old he is. And the locket proves
it. It states the year of death.

FIFTY   You don't convince me. The dead don't speak and the
Keeper could lie.

FRIEND   The Keeper lie? But he is an official, publicly sworn. His
whole function is to read the contents of the lockets
truthfully and to make them known.

FIFTY   He could be sworn to a lie.

MAN   I seem to know you.

WOMAN   I have often seen you.

MAN   If only I knew where I'd seen you.

WOMAN   Think a little. Perhaps you'll come to it.

MAN   I *am* thinking.

WOMAN   But you don't remember?

MAN   I'm very sorry. I'm not uncivil by nature.

WOMAN   Oh no. On the contrary. Shall I help you a little?

MAN   That would be very generous of you.

WOMAN   You are Professor Forty-Six.

MAN   Yes, certainly I am. You know my name.

WOMAN   I know it and honour it.

MAN   You – now I know. You are the lady in the front row.

WOMAN   Perhaps. Go on.

MAN   No, no. That's it. You always sit in the front row. I remember your eyes. You look at me in such a strange way. I don't know why it is, but one doesn't forget it.

WOMAN   I thought you hadn't noticed me at all. You always seem engrossed in your subject.

MAN   And I am. But the way you look at one struck me long ago. It is different.

WOMAN   In what way?

MAN   I don't know you otherwise at all. May I ask your name?

WOMAN   My name is Forty-Three.

MAN   Forty-Three. Then we are very close to each other.

WOMAN   I knew that long ago, Dr. Forty-Six.

MAN   Tell me, does such a thing mean so much to you too?

WOMAN   More than I can put into words. That is why I have
always sat in the front row.

MAN   Did you come only because of the name?

WOMAN   Yes, but I've gone on coming.

MAN   Also because of the name?

WOMAN   Yes.

MAN   But you weren't disappointed?

WOMAN   Oh no! I had to see you again.

MAN   Have you listened to me at all?

WOMAN   Yes. I have listened to you too. But I must admit that I
have thought about you more.

MAN   About me? What is there to think so much about?

WOMAN   Your destiny. It was an obsession. How long had he to
go on talking? How long, how long, how long? I could
think of nothing else. I've said it now. Now you will despise
me.

MAN   Have you always had such thoughts?

WOMAN   Oh no. Only since I saw you.

MAN   It astonishes me. My name is really nothing out of the
ordinary. On the contrary, I was always made to feel sorry
about this – middling – name.

WOMAN   Oh, I know. I understand very well.

MAN   And then, have you never thought of some fine young
man?

WOMAN   A young Eighty-Eight you mean?

MAN   Yes, someone quite high. All women go after them.

WOMAN   No, I've always despised that. Eighty-Eights are stupid and conceited. There's one I've been introduced to over and over again and he doesn't even recognize me. Hasn't once said good morning to me. I can't stand such arrogance.

MAN   There are so few of them. – But as a girl you must have been different – Surely it impressed you then?

WOMAN   Never, I swear. I never understood other girls. What has a man like that achieved? His eighty-eight years were hung round his neck at birth and that is all. He need only promenade his name and amuse himself. Everything else just comes to him.

MAN   That is true.

WOMAN   I don't like frivolous men. I like people whose names make things difficult for them. A man like you thinks. You *have* to think, otherwise you can achieve nothing.

MAN   But an eighty-eight has so much more time. Imagine what such a man could do if he wanted to.

WOMAN   I don't believe it. They are all heartless. They *have* to be heartless.

MAN   Why actually?

WOMAN   First of all because a man like that knows one thing for certain: he will outlive everyone round him. Not only his parents and people of an older generation – that is natural; but also his brothers and sisters, his friends, his colleagues, his wives and generally his children too. His life begins with this, with his saying this to himself. How can he love anyone? How can he give his heart to anyone? He can't know pity and he can't help anyone. His years belong to him. He can't give them away. But he doesn't want to either, for he will naturally be as hard as if he were the only man in the world. And for that he will be admired! I detest eighty-eights! I hate eighty-eights!

MAN   You are an unusual woman.

WOMAN   Perhaps I am. I will not outlive the man I love. But neither will I have him outlive me. That's not just being jealous as perhaps you think.

MAN   No, it's a very sound instinct.

WOMAN   One should begin life together and end it together. I
have sworn to myself that I will not marry a man who is
going to die before my eyes. But neither will I marry a man
who is going to watch how I die. The idea revolts me.

MAN   You want a double floor under your feet. It's not enough for
you to know about yourself.

WOMAN   No. I want to know my husband as well as I know
myself.

MAN   You seek, if you will allow me to say it, the *identical
moment.*

WOMAN   The identical moment.

MAN   That's why you sit in the front row?

WOMAN   Yes.

MAN   To see if this is it?

WOMAN   Yes.

MAN   Will you always sit in the front row?

WOMAN   Yes.

MAN   Will you still be there when you know it?

WOMAN   Yes.

MAN   And when you are his wife?

WOMAN   Yes.

MAN   With the same eyes?

WOMAN   Yes. Yes.

KEEPER   I see them all. I am appointed for that. There must be no mistake. The safety and continuance of society depend on the fact that each abides by his moment. That is the contract. The contract is tied round the neck of each man at birth. Each man grows up amongst his fellows and lives amongst them. Each man enjoys the advantages of this common life. Not everyone earns them. But to each have so many years been appointed and that number is immutable.

FIFTY   Do you never have accidents then? Suppose someone is involved in a railway crash before his moment?

KEEPER   Nothing happens to him then.

FIFTY   But how is that?

KEEPER   That, precisely, is my concern. You have interrupted me. You want to discover the truth. How can you discover the truth unless you can listen?

FIFTY   I am rather impatient. It is an exciting question. Excuse my impatience, but this question excites me intensely.

KEEPER   This question is no more important or more exciting than many others. It is a problem which has been solved to the general satisfaction. So long as I am here, there will be no confusion.

FIFTY   And when you are not here?

KEEPER   Another will be in my place, sworn to the Holy Law.

FIFTY   I have interrupted you before. You said that each man was held to his contract.

KEEPER   Yes, each man. And each man knows why. Men have learnt that fifty certain years are worth more than an indefinite number which are not certain.

FIFTY   How do you know my name? You said my name.

KEEPER   I have an instinct for names. One learns certain things in our position.

FIFTY   Can you read *every* man's name in his face?

KEEPER   Generally I can. If I am not quite sure, I refrain from guessing.

FIFTY   What then do you need the lockets for? When you are summoned to a dead man, a look is enough to tell you his age.

KEEPER   That is so. But the ritual to which I am sworn requires more.

FIFTY   Has it ever happened that someone has lost his locket?

KEEPER   You ask too much.

FIFTY   You promised to answer all my questions.

KEEPER   Nonetheless, you ask too much. Do you insist on an answer?

FIFTY   Yes. I want to know.

KEEPER   It has happened.

FIFTY   That is terrible.

KEEPER   Does it astonish you to know that even we have criminals among us?

FIFTY   Criminals?

KEEPER   Criminals! The worst crime that a man can commit is to destroy the evidence of his contract. By it alone he lives; without it he would be nothing. Whoever loses his locket steals years that are not due to him. As if it would profit him.

FIFTY   But he could just lose it, bathing or in a fire.

KEEPER   That is unlikely. For everyone knows that, without a locket, he ought not to live and, if it is lost or destroyed, he must, on pain of death, surrender himself. Anyone who does not, outlaws himself from society. He who would live without a locket is a murderer.

FIFTY   So that is a murderer. I always imagined a murderer as
        something different.

KEEPER   What you imagined was long ago. Today no one can kill
         another unless he happens to strike him at his moment.
         But, even if he so strikes him, he is not truly responsible for
         his death, for he would, in any case, have died at that
         moment.

FIFTY   How strange! But why are the locketless called murderers.

KEEPER   That can only be explained historically. At the beginning
         of this memorable epoch, it so happened that violent men
         from the scum of the people set on other men to steal their
         lockets. And many then died from fright. Thus acts of
         violence against lockets received the stigma of murder.
         Then, in the course of years, the same expression came to
         be used of those who destroyed their own lockets.

FIFTY   It seems, really, that there is nothing more sacred.

KEEPER   There is nothing more sacred. Have you not understood
         that yet?

FIFTY   I am beginning to understand it. But what happens now
        when you come across someone who has just died who
        has no locket?

KEEPER   Try to answer that for yourself.

FIFTY   You guess the age of the dead. You manage without the
        locket. You hide the fact that you have found nothing and
        you write in the register what your practised eye tells you.

KEEPER   Do you think that would be wrong?

FIFTY   What should I say? But it seems that I have guessed right.

KEEPER   (*Is silent*)

FIFTY   And if by any chance you made a mistake in such a case?
        You are called to someone who has just died. You look for
        the locket. Your hands are certainly skilful. It is as if you
        had to find something valuable on the body – in the old
        days it would have been called robbing a corpse, but we live
        in a higher civilization – so you quickly search those

31

remnants of a man and soon, perhaps in half a minute, you know that there is no locket. You are perplexed, for surely it doesn't happen often.

KEEPER   Very seldom, thank God.

FIFTY   But your perplexity could confuse your judgement. It could be that you were frightened. You come to some man who has been highly regarded during his life, one perhaps who has rendered great services to his fellow men and, in front of everyone, in front of his relatives, his friends, his admirers, you discover that this great man, honoured and world–famous, was a murderer. That might frighten anyone. That might frighten even an official of your standing and experience.

KEEPER   Why should I deny it? It has always frightened me.

FIFTY   It must frighten you very much. It must throw you into a panic, for at that moment, everything depends on your judgement. Perhaps your eye is deceived. Perhaps you are ill.

KEEPER   And suppose all that were true, what follows from it?

FIFTY   That perhaps you judge the age wrong; that, in one case at least, you are not absolutely certain whether the man has died at the right point in time. For once the contract might not hold.

KEEPER   The contract holds always. I may fail. I hold a high and noble office, but I am no God. I may fail. The contract never fails.

FIFTY   But that is not what I want to know. You are in duty bound to believe in the validity of the contract, but you cannot say that its accuracy is proved in each single case.

KEEPER   I cannot say that. But it is superfluous.

FIFTY   Nothing is superfluous. For if it could be proved that there have been mistakes in the contract, it could also happen that a man outlived his name.

KEEPER   I refuse to listen any longer. You are in the right way to become a murderer. Your flesh itches under the locket. Soon it will burn. You are not the first to end his days as a common murderer. I warn you. It is a pity about you. It is lamentable.

FIFTY   My locket does not burn my flesh. You will find it there. I know that your private name is One Hundred and Twenty-Two. Be calm. You will find my locket in its place. My name burns me. Every name burns me. Death burns me.

GRANDMOTHER AND GRAND-DAUGHTER

GRAND-DAUGHTER   And where did all the people go then, Grandma?

GRANDMOTHER   They went onto a ship, but the ship was very full. The captain said "I have too many passengers." But the people were in despair. They wanted to get away from the dangerous place, and the captain was sorry for them. He had a kind heart and he thought of his own children at home. So he let them all come on board and, when the people in the other villages saw how kind the captain was, they all came running and begged and wept and the captain gave way and let them all come. But there really were too many and when the ship reached deep water they began to be afraid. A storm was coming up and the waves were black and the people were thrown from side to side of the ship. The captain saw that they would all be lost unless the ship was lightened. He called out in a mighty voice. "We are all lost. Twenty-four passengers must jump overboard. Volunteers forward! Who will sacrifice himself for the rest?" But that was not at all easy, for the waves ran high and no one dared jump into the water.

GRAND-DAUGHTER   The water was too wet for them, wasn't it, Grandma?

GRANDMOTHER   And it was dangerous. It was certain death.

GRAND-DAUGHTER   It was certain death. What does that mean, Grandma?

GRANDMOTHER   That was in the old, old days. Then, when something dangerous happened, people died at once.

GRAND-DAUGHTER   At once?

GRANDMOTHER   Yes, at once.

GRAND-DAUGHTER   But then it was their moment, Grandma?

GRANDMOTHER   No, not exactly. In those days it could happen at any time. People didn't know when. A little girl went for a walk in the street and fell and hit her head and died.

GRAND-DAUGHTER   That must have hurt her. I've hurt myself too.

GRANDMOTHER   But you always get better. In those days, people didn't always get better. Then you could hurt yourself so much that you died.

GRAND-DAUGHTER   I can't hurt myself so much, can I Grandma?

GRANDMOTHER   No, you can't.

GRAND-DAUGHTER   Suppose I was run over?

GRANDMOTHER   You might lose a leg.

GRAND-DAUGHTER   Then I'd only have one leg?

GRANDMOTHER   Then you'd only have one leg and you'd get another leg made of wood so that no one would notice any more.

GRAND-DAUGHTER   And then I'd live happily for ever?

GRANDMOTHER   Not for ever. Till your moment.

GRAND-DAUGHTER   Grandma, what is my moment?

GRANDMOTHER   Now you know that. I've told you that so often.

GRAND-DAUGHTER   I've forgotten.

GRANDMOTHER   You haven't forgotten at all.

GRAND-DAUGHTER   But I *have* forgotten.

GRANDMOTHER   You just say that because you want me to tell you again, little fraud.

GRAND-DAUGHTER   Please, I am a fraud. But if I say I'm a fraud, then tell me when is my moment.

GRANDMOTHER   You should tell me.

GRAND-DAUGHTER   I can't count.

GRANDMOTHER   But you must learn.

GRAND-DAUGHTER   You help me.

GRANDMOTHER   I'll help you, but you must do some of the work yourself.

GRAND-DAUGHTER   All right. We'll count together.

GRANDMOTHER   And what happened to the people on the ship? Don't you want to know any more?

GRAND-DAUGHTER   Oh, I think those were stupid people.

GRANDMOTHER   Stupid? Why were they stupid.

GRAND-DAUGHTER   They didn't know about themselves. They didn't trust themselves in the water. They were frightened of the water. I'd jump in the water at once.

GRANDMOTHER   But nothing would happen to you.

GRAND-DAUGHTER   People in the old days were stupid. It's just a fairy story.

GRANDMOTHER   But you like fairy stories.

GRAND-DAUGHTER   I only like them about clever people. Could the captain have jumped in the water?

GRANDMOTHER   He could have.

GRAND-DAUGHTER   Would anything have happened to him?

GRANDMOTHER   Yes, of course something would have happened to him. He would have drowned. It was like that then. If no one rescued you, you drowned.

GRAND-DAUGHTER   You see, even the captain! That was a stupid time.

GRANDMOTHER   You'd rather live now, wouldn't you?

GRAND-DAUGHTER   I'd much, much rather live now, Grandma. There are no giants or ogres now and people aren't always drowning. You know when your moment is, don't you, Grandma?

GRANDMOTHER   Yes, of course I do. Everyone knows that, child.

GRAND-DAUGHTER   Tell me it. Tell me. Tell me. Please, please tell me. I want to know it. Tell me. I'll always be good at school. I'll always pay attention. I'll never take things out of the larder again if you tell me. I'll never tell a lie again. Please tell me, please, please.

GRANDMOTHER   What has come over you, little idiot? Nobody tells that. What do you think would happen if people knew? They'd all stare at one.

GRAND-DAUGHTER   But why, Grandma? I know mine.

GRANDMOTHER   But everyone keeps it to themselves. Nobody speaks of it. It's a secret. A child might talk about it, but only a child. No grown-up would do such a thing. It wouldn't be right. It would be a scandal.

GRAND-DAUGHTER   Grandma, If I don't tell anyone – am I grown up then?

GRANDMOTHER   Yes, if you never speak of it again to anyone, if you keep it absolutely to yourself, then you're grown up.

GRAND-DAUGHTER   Suppose I talk to you about it?

GRANDMOTHER   If you really can't keep it to yourself, it's better that you should talk to me. But, one day, you will be so grown up that you won't talk about it to anyone. Then you will be really grown up.

GRAND-DAUGHTER   Not to anyone at all? Not to anyone in the whole world?

GRANDMOTHER   Not to anyone in the whole world.

GRAND-DAUGHTER   Not even to my doll?

GRANDMOTHER   Not even to your doll.

GRAND-DAUGHTER   Grandma, I'll begin today. I know exactly when my moment is. Do you think I know?

GRANDMOTHER   Of course I think so.

GRAND-DAUGHTER   I won't count up any more, not even with you. I'm quite grown up already, aren't I? Am I grown up enough?

GRANDMOTHER   Yes. Now you are.

FIFTY IS CROSSING THE STREET. A STONE HITS HIM ON THE HEAD. THEN ANOTHER, THEN A THIRD AND A FOURTH

FIFTY   Who's that throwing stones? Who's throwing stones at me? Hi, what does this mean? Will you stop? Just wait till I catch you. I'll give it to you. I'll get you. Stop, I say, stop! What a thing to do. (*He sees a boy behind a pillar*) Oh it's you! Where are the others? How dare you?

BOY   I haven't done anything.

FIFTY   What have you got in your hand?

BOY   (*Quickly dropping two stones*) Nothing.

FIFTY   No. You've just dropped two stones.

BOY   I didn't throw any.

FIFTY   Who did then? Where are the others?

BOY   There aren't any others.

FIFTY   You've no friends?

BOY   No, I'm all alone.

FIFTY   Then you did throw the stones?

BOY   I didn't do anything.

FIFTY   You're a liar too. If you throw stones, you should also have the courage to own up. Otherwise you're a coward.

BOY   I'm not a coward.

FIFTY   Then admit that you threw the stones.

BOY   I did throw them.

FIFTY   That's better. And why did you throw them?

BOY   Because I'm allowed to.

FIFTY   What do you mean? Why are you allowed to throw stones?

BOY   I'm allowed to. I'm allowed to do everything.

FIFTY   And who allows you to do that?

BOY   My mother.

FIFTY   You expect me to believe that? You're lying again.

BOY   I'm not lying. I'm not a coward.

FIFTY   Then I'll ask your parents. Take me to them.

BOY   (*Comes forward, puts his hand in Fifty's and says trustingly*) I'll take you to them. Will you come with me? It's quite near.

FIFTY   Aren't you frightened of your parents?

BOY   Oh no. I'm not frightened. I'm not frightened of anyone.

FIFTY   But you'll be punished. I shall tell them what you've done.

BOY   You come. You can tell them. My mother never does
        anything to me. My father never does anything to me either.

FIFTY   You're a strange boy.

BOY   Why am I strange?

FIFTY   What does your teacher say when you throw stones?

BOY   I haven't got a teacher.

FIFTY   But you go to school. There's a teacher there.

BOY   I don't go to school. I have no teacher.

FIFTY   And I'm to believe that? Boys of your age always go to
        school.

BOY   But I don't.

FIFTY   Then why not? Are you ill?

BOY   Oh no. I'm not ill.

FIFTY   I should hardly have thought you were after your stone-
        throwing. You look quite healthy to me.

BOY   I'm never ill.

FIFTY   Then why don't you go to school?

BOY   Because I don't want to.

FIFTY   And don't your parents want you to go to school?

BOY   Oh no.

FIFTY   Can you read and write?

BOY   No. I don't like it.

FIFTY   Don't your parents want you to learn to read and write?

BOY   I don't want to. I don't feel like it.

FIFTY   And what will you do when you're grown up?

BOY   (*Remains silent*)

FIFTY   Have you never thought of that? All the other boys will be able to read books and everyone will laugh at you.

BOY   (*Remains silent*)

FIFTY   Don't you mind when people laugh at you?

BOY   They don't laugh at me at all.

FIFTY   But when you're older. Everyone will think that you're stupid.

BOY   But I'm not stupid.

FIFTY   Then you must prove it. That's why boys go to school.

BOY   I don't have to.

FIFTY   What *do* you have to do?

BOY   I don't have to do anything.

FIFTY   And that's why you're allowed to throw stones! You stand in the street and throw stones all day long.

BOY   I'm allowed to do anything.

FIFTY   You're the strangest boy I ever met. What's your name?

BOY   My name is *Ten*.

TWO COLLEAGUES

FIRST COLLEAGUE   I can't get it done.

SECOND COLLEAGUE   You don't try hard enough.

FIRST COLLEAGUE   But I drive myself. I try in every possible way. I work the whole day and half the night as well. I hardly eat. I hardly sleep. You can see for yourself that I've taken on too much.

SECOND COLLEAGUE   Yes, when I look at you properly, I must say that you're right. You don't look at all well. You're working far too hard.

FIRST COLLEAGUE   And yet I tell you, I can't get it done.

SECOND COLLEAGUE   But how is that? Perhaps you are too ambitious.

FIRST COLLEAGUE   I can't manage it. I shan't finish it.

SECOND COLLEAGUE   But that depends on yourself.

FIRST COLLEAGUE   It's easy to say that.

SECOND COLLEAGUE   Are you disturbed? Do you not get sufficient peace to work?

FIRST COLLEAGUE   I have perfect peace. I couldn't ask for better conditions to work in.

SECOND COLLEAGUE   I don't understand it. What are you complaining about then?

FIRST COLLEAGUE   I haven't enough time.

SECOND COLLEAGUE   But why?

FIRST COLLEAGUE   Have you ever considered how old I might be?

SECOND COLLEAGUE   No. I never do that. I hate indiscretion. I never rack my brains over how old my friends may be. It is a secret and should remain a secret. I have far too much respect for a man's personality to pry into such things. A human being to me is something inviolable.

FIRST COLLEAGUE   But you know my name.

SECOND COLLEAGUE   Of course. We all know that. I can't stop my ears to what is generally known. I know how old you will be when you die, but I don't know how old you are. That is a secret. It pleases me very much that everyone should have this secret of his own. It gives one freedom to arrange one's life as one thinks best.

FIRST COLLEAGUE   You think so?

SECOND COLLEAGUE   Yes. No one can prescribe to you what you should do with yourself because no one knows how long you have to live. But you know it and can live accordingly. You are born with a fixed capital of years. It will neither be diminished nor added to. No one can steal any part of it. It belongs inalienably to your name. You can't throw it away, for you get it only year by year. You alone know how much you have, so that no one can interfere. Everything depends on you yourself cutting your coat according to your cloth. If you know how to do that, you will make something of your life. But you must know what to buy with your time. It is your own fault if you lay it out badly.

FIRST COLLEAGUE   But one may undertake some large work and simply not be able to finish it.

SECOND COLLEAGUE   Then you have over-reached yourself. That is your own fault. One should make a rough estimate before one begins.

FIRST COLLEAGUE   But there are things which can't be measured out. A piece of work can grow as one does it.

SECOND COLLEAGUE   Then one has to revise one's plan and reduce it.

FIRST COLLEAGUE   I can't do that. It's become part of me. I must go on with it as I have begun.

SECOND COLLEAGUE   Then no one can help you.

FIRST COLLEAGUE   It torments me more than I can say. I see my end clearly and I know for certain that I shall not finish.

SECOND COLLEAGUE   That is very regrettable.

FIRST COLLEAGUE   You see, you don't know how old I already am. I've always looked younger than my age. It's terrible how deceptive that is.

42

SECOND COLLEAGUE   Really.

FIRST COLLEAGUE   I shall tell you. I shall tell you my age. You'll
    be astonished.

SECOND COLLEAGUE   But I don't want to know it.

FIRST COLLEAGUE   But if I tell you of my own free will?

SECOND COLLEAGUE   I don't want to know it. I have already
    said that I hate indiscretion. It is sad enough that a man
    should have got so far and want to give away his greatest
    secret. But I do not wish to be an accomplice. I keep myself
    clear of such things.

FIRST COLLEAGUE   It would be a great relief to me. Perhaps it
    might frighten you a little. But you would understand why I
    am so disturbed. I *cannot* finish under these conditions. I
    want to tell you.

SECOND COLLEAGUE   I forbid you to tell me any such thing.
    Your age does not interest me, nor should I be frightened. I
    refuse to be frightened about such things. It is criminal to
    trouble another, even a friend, with such private matters.
    Keep your years to yourself.

FIRST COLLEAGUE   If only it was years.

SECOND COLLEAGUE   You are shameless. I refuse to
    understand your implication. There are, of course, people
    who lie and try to impress their friends with fantastic
    confessions about their age. It's a form of showing off with
    which you, no doubt, are familiar.

FIRST COLLEAGUE   But you wrong me terribly. I just wanted to
    tell someone, but no one will listen. Everyone runs away
    when I try. Is it so terrible to know how old a man is?

SECOND COLLEAGUE   No. It may not be so terrible in itself. But
    the reason, the reason that drives you to tell it, that is
    terrible. You want to complain about having to die so soon.
    You want to sow discord amongst men. You would like
    everyone to be as discontented as yourself.

FIRST COLLEAGUE   But why should I do that? I am only

thinking of my work.

SECOND COLLEAGUE   You don't believe that yourself. I know
that trick. You go about looking for a victim. You are too
weak to bear quietly what everyone bears. You are a
coward, and contemptible. You fear your moment. You are
a monstrosity.

FIRST COLLEAGUE   A coward, and contemptible. A monstrosity.
I fear my moment.

THE COUPLE

SHE   So soon!

HE   But we shall see each other again?

SHE   Shall we see each other again?

HE   Yes. We love each other.

SHE   But shall we see each other again?

HE   Weren't you happy?

SHE   Happy – Oh – happy! .

HE   Then you will come again.

SHE   I don't know.

HE   You hurt me. How can you hurt me like this?

SHE   I don't want to hurt you. I love you very much.

HE   Then tell me when you will come again.

SHE   I don't know.

HE   You must know.

SHE   Don't keep on. I can't tell you.

HE   Why can't you tell me? What prevents you?

SHE   Don't ask so much.

HE   But I can't live unless I know when you will come again. I must
       know. I *will* know. I won't let you go unless you tell me. I'll
       shut you up here. I won't let you go. I'll keep you a
       prisoner.

SHE   That won't help you.

HE   You won't let me keep you?

SHE   No.

HE   And everything was so wonderful till now. You came to me. I
       have never loved anyone so much as I love you.

SHE   That's what one says. That's what one thinks.

HE   I don't say it. I don't think it. I know it. I can't live without you.

SHE   You will have to try.

HE   I know I can't.

SHE   One can do more than one thinks.

HE   Perhaps I could do better if I knew why you won't come back.

SHE   Are you sure it would be easier for you then?

HE   Yes. It could never be easy. It breaks my heart. But perhaps
       there is a reason why you can't. Perhaps it's not in your
       power.

SHE   That is it. It is not in my power. I cannot see you again.

HE   Perhaps you only think that. Perhaps I can do something. I
       would do anything to see you again. Anything. Only tell me.
       Tell me.

SHE   There is nothing you can do.

HE   That's never true. If a man wants, he can do anything.

Everything is in our power. Everything.

SHE   That's what children think.

HE   You came today. You made it possible today. Why not tomorrow? Why not tomorrow?

SHE   Tomorrow is not possible.

HE   Then the day after. I shall think about you the whole day tomorrow. If only I can see you the day after. I shall stay awake. I won't sleep for two nights. I shall see you in front of me all the time, without stopping. I shan't let your image go from me for a moment if only you will come then.

SHE   Moment.

HE   (*Frightened*) Moment. Why do you say that? What do you mean?

SHE   I said nothing.

HE   But you did. You said something terrible.

SHE   What did I say?

HE   I . . . I can't remember.

SHE   I said nothing.

HE   Moment.

SHE   That's what I *thought*. Did I say it?

HE   Yes. What did you mean?

SHE   I didn't want to frighten you.

HE   Nothing can frighten me. Only tell me. Only tell me.

SHE   Tomorrow is my birthday.

HE   Your birthday?

SHE   My *last* birthday – do you understand?

HE   Your last birthday. Why did you do it?

SHE   That's why I came. That's why I came to you.

FIFTY AND A YOUNG WOMAN AT THE FUNERAL OF HER CHILD

FIFTY   Young woman, young woman! I must speak to you. Don't be frightened, young woman. I don't know who you are. I don't even know your name. But I know that this is the funeral of your child. Answer me, I beg you, young woman. Answer me. You have lost your child?

YOUNG WOMAN   Yes.

FIFTY   He was very young?

YOUNG WOMAN   Yes.

FIFTY   How old was he?

YOUNG WOMAN   Seven.

FIFTY   You are very unhappy?

YOUNG WOMAN   No.

FIFTY   You loved him very much?

YOUNG WOMAN   Yes.

FIFTY   And you are not very unhappy?

YOUNG WOMAN   No. Not at all.

FIFTY   Why not?

YOUNG WOMAN   I knew when he would die. I always knew it.

FIFTY   But then you were very unhappy when he was alive?

YOUNG WOMAN   No.

FIFTY   Aren't you at all sorry that he had to die so young?

YOUNG WOMAN   I knew it from the time he was born.

FIFTY   Would you have liked to prevent it?

YOUNG WOMAN   One can't do that.

FIFTY   Did you try?

YOUNG WOMAN   No. Nobody does that.

FIFTY   But suppose you were the first person to try?

YOUNG WOMAN   Me? Just me? No.

FIFTY   You'd never be the only person to do something?

YOUNG WOMAN   I should have been ashamed.

FIFTY   Ashamed? Why?

YOUNG WOMAN   People would have pointed me out. They would have said, "She's not right in the head."

FIFTY   But if you could have saved him? If you had managed to keep him alive for another year?

YOUNG WOMAN   (*Indignant*) That's robbery. That's a crime.

FIFTY   Why is it a crime?

YOUNG WOMAN   It's blasphemy.

FIFTY   Why is it blasphemy?

YOUNG WOMAN   His time was settled beforehand. A year!

FIFTY   Can you picture such a year to yourself?

YOUNG WOMAN   (*More and more indignant*) I should have been terrified the whole time. I should have felt unnatural with the child. I should have thought I'd stolen my own child. I've never stolen and I shan't ever steal. I'm an honest woman. I should have had to keep him hidden. People would have looked at me as if I had something stolen in the house.

FIFTY   But he was your child. How can you steal your own child?

YOUNG WOMAN   I should have stolen the year. It didn't belong to him. He was seven. He was called Seven. A year, a whole year, with such a thing on my conscience.

FIFTY   And if it had only been a month?

YOUNG WOMAN   I can't imagine it. The more I think about it, the more dreadful it seems.

FIFTY   And a day? One single day? Suppose you had been able to keep him one single day longer? A day. A day is so short.

YOUNG WOMAN   You frighten me. You are the tempter. You have come to lead me into temptation. But I won't listen to you. A day! A whole day! I should have thought every minute that they'd come for me. I always fed him well. I always looked after him properly. He was beautifully dressed. He looked nicer than any of the other children. People praised him. They admired him. Everything was always done properly for him. Anyone will tell you that. Ask them here at the funeral. Ask the neighbours. Ask all the neighbours if you don't believe me. I did everything that a mother should. I didn't neglect anything. Many a night I couldn't sleep because of him calling me. I never said a cross word to him. I loved him so. Anyone will tell you that.

FIFTY   I believe you. I believe you.

THE YOUNG MEN

FIRST YOUNG MAN   What shall we do today?

SECOND YOUNG MAN   What shall we do today? The same, I suppose, as we always do.

FIRST YOUNG MAN   And that is?

SECOND YOUNG MAN   I give you one guess.

FIRST YOUNG MAN   What do you think?

SECOND YOUNG MAN   Nothing.

FIRST YOUNG MAN   Correct. Nothing. It always is nothing.

SECOND YOUNG MAN   It always was nothing.

FIRST YOUNG MAN   And it always will be nothing.

SECOND YOUNG MAN   That is life.

FIRST YOUNG MAN   Oh the boredom! The boredom!

SECOND YOUNG MAN   There was always that.

FIRST YOUNG MAN   It can't have been so boring in the past.

SECOND YOUNG MAN   Why not?

FIRST YOUNG MAN   Because no one could have stood it.

SECOND YOUNG MAN   And what was so *different* then? There have always been men, always after the same lamentable idiocies, the same appetites, occasionally dressed up grand.

FIRST YOUNG MAN   But of course it was quite different. Can you imagine what it meant to *kill* someone?

SECOND YOUNG MAN   No, I can't. We're past such barbarous folly.

FIRST YOUNG MAN   Folly! Folly! I'd give a lot to be able to kill someone.

SECOND YOUNG MAN   What stops you?

FIRST YOUNG MAN   What stops me? Everything. I know too much. I know that it's not in my hands whether the man I hit dies or not. If I hit him at the right moment, well, he would have died anyway and I haven't killed him. If I hit him at the wrong moment, he doesn't die. Whatever I do, his death does not depend on me. The most worthless man in the world is safe from me.

SECOND YOUNG MAN   That is true. But isn't it precisely that that we're so proud of?

FIRST YOUNG MAN   Proud, yes. But I hanker after the time when a man could confront his enemy and in due form, despatch him. Can you imagine that? A *duel*.

SECOND YOUNG MAN   Ah, that must have been beautiful.

FIRST YOUNG MAN   You never knew what would happen. Nothing was certain. You might be hit, or the other man might be hit.

SECOND YOUNG MAN   Often no one was hit.

FIRST YOUNG MAN   So much the better. Then one could go and challenge someone else.

SECOND YOUNG MAN   Sometimes someone would be hit.

FIRST YOUNG MAN   And if you hit him, you knew you had killed him, you yourself and only you. It was plain that you had killed the man.

SECOND YOUNG MAN   But afterwards? Then you had to hide or fly. You were a murderer.

FIRST YOUNG MAN   Well, why not? I should like to be such a murderer. I should at least know why I was called murderer.

SECOND YOUNG MAN   Not like today.

FIRST YOUNG MAN   Today? What is a murderer today? A common locket thief. That's a murderer. His victim runs round as gay as ever, but he is grandly called "Murderer". You know, that shocks me. If one can't kill anyone, then one should at least let the word for it rest in peace.

SECOND YOUNG MAN   I've thought that too. But so it is.

FIRST YOUNG MAN   The fatal thing is, that one can't do anything about it. One is tied hand and foot. Since one can't kill anyone, one can't ever alter anything either.

SECOND YOUNG MAN   You're right. I never thought of that.

FIRST YOUNG MAN   So everything will be for ever as it is now.

SECOND YOUNG MAN   For ever. And you will never be able to kill anyone.

FIRST YOUNG MAN   Never. It's too stupid.

THE TWO LADIES

FIRST LADY   What would you give her? You're such a good judge.

SECOND LADY   A year, I'd say. A bare year.

FIRST LADY   You think she's still got a year?

SECOND LADY   A bare year. Perhaps only six months.

FIRST LADY   She gives out that she's got more. Sometimes she says six years to me, sometimes seven.

SECOND LADY   Fantastic! She just wants that to get round.

FIRST LADY   Well, she always tells me as a secret and begs me not to betray her.

SECOND LADY   She counts on your being indiscreet.

FIRST LADY   You know she's still hoping for a man?

SECOND LADY   What? When she's only got a year? Don't make me laugh. A man wouldn't touch her. One year! No man would have her. Even if she was a raving beauty, no one would have her with one year. If you were a man would you take on a woman who had one year?

FIRST LADY   A lot of men would be glad to, you know.

SECOND LADY   I know these short men. A woman with any self-respect keeps clear of them. To me short men are animals.

FIRST LADY   There are very attractive short men, you know. I have a cousin who has just got married again to another low woman. He says it's just prejudice. It's the only kind he'd ever marry. When she dies, he'll certainly marry another low woman. A low woman takes more trouble to leave pleasant memories behind her. A low woman wants to live well because she can't wait. A low woman, he says, is always in a secret panic. She knows she's got no more coming, and so she's content with what she has. A low woman is less demanding.

SECOND LADY   But that's all nonsense. A low woman wants to

52

enjoy life because she doesn't know any better. She wants new lovers, new clothes. She's extravagant. What does it matter to her what happens afterwards?

FIRST LADY   That's what *I* thought. My cousin says I'm wrong though. He has just, for the fourth time, married another low woman. His motto is: Hands off high women! Imagine, he says, that it's a bad marriage, and she's a high woman. Whether the man can stick it or not, there she is, with a claim on him, for goodness knows how long.

SECOND LADY   And suppose he's happy now with a low woman and it comes to an end soon, has he considered that he'll then be empty handed and will have to look for a new one? I'll admit that there are some decent low women. But then it's even worse for a man who's had to do with one of them. The next won't be like that, you can believe me.

FIRST LADY   He says that, if one is experienced, one is all right. He chooses very carefully. He's already chosen the next. She's even lower, he says. He's not quite decided on the next after that, but he has someone in sight.

SECOND LADY   He works it all out while the others are still alive?

FIRST LADY   Of course. That's the great advantage. He picks them very carefully. How long do I want to live with the next, he asks himself, and, once he's clear about that, he can look round and decide.

SECOND LADY   But, good heavens, do all these women wait for him?

FIRST LADY   Of course. If he's engaged to them. He's fantastically attractive. They'd all wait ten years for him. But it's never so long. He has a wonderful life. He's determined to run through twenty marriages.

SECOND LADY   I think that's excessive. How does he *know* how old his brides are?

FIRST LADY   He's got a very good eye, you know. He would have, naturally, with his experience. It's a kind of game to him, guessing the right age. He's in such demand that a lot of women tell him their age straightaway, of their own accord.

SECOND WOMAN   I wouldn't do that for any man. They must be shameless.

FIRST LADY   You were never crazy enough.

SECOND LADY   And do none of them lie to him?

FIRST LADY   It happens. Many make themselves out older, from jealousy.

SECOND LADY   From jealousy?

FIRST LADY   Yes. There was one who gave him to understand that she had two years left, and on that understanding, he married her. Of course, she was terribly in love with him. They always are. It was agreed that he should look round for her successor meanwhile. She could hardly bear the idea, but she must have agreed to it or he wouldn't have married her. He, as his custom is, had a good look round and found someone to suit him for the next. She pledged herself, regarded herself as engaged and waited – though not patiently. His wife's last birthday arrived and he, kindly and tactfully – he's not a monster you know – assumed that she would die. He waited the whole day, waited till late into the night. Nothing happened. He went to bed and thought: By the time I wake up in the morning it will be over. My wife won't be getting up again. But, next morning he opened his eyes and there she was, wagging her head and plodding thoughtfully up and down the bedroom. "Darling, what does this mean?" he said to her, "I made a mistake", she said. "I'm younger than I thought. It's not till next year." There was nothing he could do. He knew that she'd lied to him, but there she was for another whole year to the extreme annoyance of her successor, who thought she'd been had. It was a ludicrous story. It went all round. You must have heard people talking about it.

SECOND LADY   It's all quite possible. He may well have an amusing life. But I don't call that love. You can say what you like, but real love only exists with high women. For real love, you need time. You have to learn to know each other, you have to experience things together, you have to learn to trust each other blindfold. Fifty years of marriage is my ideal.

FIRST LADY   So you are against low men too.

SECOND LADY   Of course I am. I'm against everything low. I'm for everything high.

FIRST LADY   You're lucky to get through life with such expectations.

SECOND LADY   I've always had them. Only the best is good enough for me. A man lower than Eighty-eight means nothing to me.

FIRST LADY   Look. By and large, you're right. But one learns to compromise. I was like you once. But what have I done in the end?

SECOND LADY   You've married a middling man.

FIRST LADY   I'm middling too.

SECOND LADY   It's just the middling that I hate most. I should have thought it much better for you to marry a quite low man – a twenty or thirty – then, later, to have been ready for a great life.

FIRST LADY   I'm a creature of habit. I get used to a man and then I don't want any other. I'm not romantic.

SECOND LADY   So I see. You're a real *middler*.

FIRST LADY   You're not so high yourself.

SECOND LADY   I'm quite content with my name. I'm fifteen years better than you anyway.

FIRST LADY   You needn't go on about it.

SECOND LADY   I don't want to annoy you, but you must realize that we think differently about a lot of things. We're quite different by temperament. I'm high, you're middle and there's nothing to be done about it.

FIFTY BEFORE THE ASSEMBLED PEOPLE. THE KEEPER, ROBED AND VESTED, STANDS NEAR HIM AND SPEAKS LOUDLY SO THAT ALL MAY HEAR.

FIFTY   It is not my moment.

KEEPER   You are wrong. Your moment has come.

FIFTY   It has not come. I know how old I am.

KEEPER   Your memory deceives you.

FIFTY   Test my memory. Test it. You will find it correct.

KEEPER   It is not for me to test your memory. Perhaps it is correct, but your moment has come.

FIFTY   How can it have come if my memory is correct and I know my age?

KEEPER   You were taught it wrong. A child is often misled. There are mothers who do not observe the law. Luckily there are not many such mothers.

FIFTY   But how do you know? How could you find out that my mother misled me?

KEEPER   I know.

FIFTY   Did she tell you? You don't know her. She is still alive. You know only the dead.

KEEPER   He blasphemes. It is time that he ceased to blaspheme.

PEOPLE   He blasphemes. He blasphemes.

KEEPER   You have profaned a burial. The law condemns you to the public moment.

FIFTY   But I ask you to delay execution for a day. You know that it must be. You are so certain. I beg for one day. I am ready to confess if you will grant me one day.

KEEPER   The law allows no delay. But it is better for you that you should confess.

FIFTY   I confess that I am fifty years old today. It is true that I have never bothered about it. I didn't admit it because it meant nothing to me. I have never believed in my moment.

KEEPER   He blasphemes. He has set himself against the Law.

PEOPLE   Lead us not into temptation. Lead us not into temptation.

FIFTY   I have confessed. Give me *one day*. I am ready to put myself at the Keeper's disposal as if I were dead. You can fetter me, you can chain me. You can deny me food. You can prevent me sleeping. Do what you will with me, but let me live one day longer. Are you not sure then? Do you perhaps tremble for your law? If the law is the truth, let us test it.

KEEPER   The Law cannot be tested. The Law is sacred.

FIFTY   It is your great, your last opportunity. Here stands one who has never believed in his moment. When will you have such a rare creature in your midst again? I don't claim any credit for it. I am nothing special. It is my passion as you have your passions. It is my passion to mistrust the moment. My passion happens to be different from yours. But it can be useful to you. It is an opportunity to see whether a man must die at his *moment, even if he does not believe in it*. I don't believe in it. Do you understand that? I don't believe in it at all.

KEEPER   This is sacrilege. He is not mad. It is a deliberate outrage as it was at the funeral. He is in his sound mind. He spoke to me like this before. I warned him. I knew how it would end.

FIFTY   If you are so certain, Keeper, grant me a day. A day is in your power. Before all the people, grant me a day.

KEEPER   A day is not in my power. Nothing is in my power.

FIFTY   That's what you say. But you know better.

KEEPER   Repent before you die. You still have time to repent. Repent.

FIFTY   I have nothing to repent. But I entreat your mercy. Grant me a day.

KEEPER   Coward. There is only one way to mercy for you. Recant and acknowledge the moment.

FIFTY   Oh, if I could. If I could. I would do it for your sake because I grieve for you.

KEEPER   You are on the right road to it. Those were the first words that I have willingly heard you speak. Those were the first human words.

FIFTY   I shall try to find more such words for you. Will you obtain mercy for me if I really repent?

KEEPER   I will try. But it does not lie well within my power.

FIFTY   You will try. Tell me, what will happen to me if I recant?

KEEPER   If you recant you will, of your own accord, die at your moment.

FIFTY   And will you then let me die in peace?

KEEPER   I will try to. But you have not much time.

FIFTY   What must I do?

KEEPER   You must recant before all the people.

FIFTY   What must I say?

KEEPER   You must repeat aloud the words which I shall say. Repeat: I believe in the Holy Law. Repeat aloud. Begin.

FIFTY   I believe in the Holy Law.

KEEPER   I believe in the moment.

FIFTY   I believe in the moment.

KEEPER   I will die as it is ordained for me.

FIFTY   I will die as it is ordained for me.

KEEPER   And as each man dies.

FIFTY   And as each man dies.

KEEPER   Each man has his moment.

FIFTY   Each man has his moment.

KEEPER   And each man knows it.

FIFTY   And each man knows it.

KEEPER   No man yet has outlived his moment.

FIFTY   No man yet has outlived his moment.

KEEPER   I thank you for your indulgence. I was blind.

FIFTY   I thank you for your indulgence. I was blind.

KEEPER   Now you are discharged.

FIFTY   Can I now go free?

KEEPER   You can. But you are no longer the same.

FIFTY   O hours, O blessed hours that I have won!

KEEPER   Do not forget that I shall see you again soon.

FIFTY   I shall see you again soon?

KEEPER   You will not see me. But I shall see you.

FIFTY   When you look for my locket.

KEEPER   Be silent.

*The next scene follows without a break. THE KEEPER AND THE
CHORUS OF THE UNEQUAL: UNEQUAL IN THAT THEIR
MOMENTS ARE DIFFERENT.*

CHORUS   We are grateful.

KEEPER   (*He sounds like a priest chanting*) Wherefore are you
          grateful?

CHORUS   We are grateful because we have no fear.

KEEPER   Wherefore have you no fear?

59

CHORUS   We have no fear because we know what lies before us.

KEEPER   Is it so desirable, that which lies before you?

CHORUS   It is not desirable. But we have no fear.

KEEPER   Wherefore have you no fear if that which lies before you is not desirable?

CHORUS   We know when. We know when.

KEEPER   Since when have you known when?

CHORUS   Since we could think.

KEEPER   Is it so desirable to know when?

CHORUS   It is desirable to know when.

KEEPER   Are you glad to be together?

CHORUS   No. We are not glad to be together.

KEEPER   Wherefore are you together, when you are not glad to be together?

CHORUS   We are together for appearance only. We shall part.

KEEPER   For what do you wait?

CHORUS   We wait for the moment that shall part us.

KEEPER   You know the moment?

CHORUS   Each man knows it. Each man knows the moment which shall part him from all others.

KEEPER   You trust your knowledge?

CHORUS   We trust it.

KEEPER   You are happy? What more do you desire?

CHORUS   We desire nothing. We are happy.

KEEPER   You are happy because you know the moment?

CHORUS   We know it. Because we know the moment we fear nothing.

KEEPER   Content. Content.

CHORUS   Content. Content. Content.

End of Part One.

PART TWO

FRIEND   It's you, I'm glad it's you.

FIFTY   Can you explain to me how I come to be alive still?

FRIEND   Have you not had warning enough? What sort of explanation are you waiting for now?

FIFTY   Then you know what happened?

FRIEND   Yes. Everyone knows. People talk of nothing else.

FIFTY   I wish you had been there.

FRIEND   I couldn't have helped you.

FIFTY   No. But you would have been a witness, there in the crowd.

FRIEND   Are you not your own witness?

FIFTY   I think I remained calm and collected. I thought of what I wanted to know, of the answer to my question. I wanted people to listen to me. I wanted them to listen for a long time. My only thought was: How can I prolong this scene?

FRIEND   And you didn't see the people? You didn't feel how they were all intent on you, how, at a word from the Keeper, they would have torn you to pieces.

FIFTY   Of course. I felt the threat. I may have been more frightened than I seemed. But I was also very curious. If they had fallen on me, if, as you say, at a word from the Keeper, they had actually torn me to pieces, would I then have died at the right point in time? Or would it have been three hours before the real moment. Or two? Or one? Can one die before one's moment?

FRIEND   But you came round in time. I am very glad that you did.

FIFTY   Why are you glad?

FRIEND   Because I am fond of you. You talk to me. You are
          there.

FIFTY   Do I mean so much to you then?

FRIEND   I thought you knew it.

FIFTY   Is that a thing one ever knows?

FRIEND   One can be told.

FIFTY   Do people mean much to you?

FRIEND   Some do.

FIFTY   Are there many who do?

FRIEND   No. Very few. Perhaps that's why they mean so much to
          me.

FIFTY   How many people do you really love?

FRIEND   I am ashamed to tell you the truth.

FIFTY   Well?

FRIEND   Don't you know it?

FIFTY   I believe that, of course, your little sister means most to
          you, her image I mean. Forgive me mentioning it.

FRIEND   I still love her. I have never got over it.

FIFTY   You never spoke of her before.

FRIEND   I couldn't. You are the only one. But through all these
          years I have thought of her. I have never told anyone.

FIFTY   And is there no one else for you? You live in mourning for
          her still?

FRIEND   Yes. As long as I had spoken to no one about it,
          everyone else was equally indifferent to me.

FIFTY   You never accepted it. Perhaps that's why I felt so drawn
          towards you.

FRIEND   I never accepted it. No.

66

FIFTY   I honour you for it.

FRIEND   Don't say that. Do you know what it means? Years and years of pain and nothing can quiet it. Nothing. Nothing.

FIFTY   But is it different now?

FRIEND   Lately it has become a little different.

FIFTY   There is someone else who means a lot to you?

FRIEND   Yes.

FIFTY   Did it happen suddenly?

FRIEND   Yes.

FIFTY   So a new person has come into your life and I, your best friend, have known nothing.

FRIEND   It is no one new. It is someone I have known for a long time.

FIFTY   But how did it happen?

FRIEND   Your curiosity is like a hungry wolf. But I can never refuse to answer you.

FIFTY   How did it happen?

FRIEND   I talked to someone about her.

FIFTY   About your sister?

FRIEND   Yes.

FIFTY   And since then you have loved the person with whom you spoke of her?

FRIEND   Yes. Nearly as much as herself.

FIFTY   But then you must also love me.

FRIEND   But you are he. You are the person I spoke to. No one else knows about it.

FIFTY   I am he. How strange.

FRIEND   You forced me to tell you the truth.

FIFTY   I hope you don't regret it. But does it surpise you? Haven't
I trusted you with what torments and pursues *me*? You
have given me your pain. And isn't what torments us the
same at bottom?

FRIEND   No. I am only concerned with this one person. I don't
mind what happens to other people.

FIFTY   But now you are concerned with me too. And I do mind
what happens to everyone.

FRIEND   That is what frightens me. I have a feeling that something
terrible could happen to you. I trembled when you were
brought before the people.

FIFTY   So you were there.

FRIEND   Yes.

FIFTY   And you didn't want to tell me?

FRIEND   No.

FIFTY   But why not?

FRIEND   I was afraid that it would encourage you in your suicidal
undertaking, just the fact that I was there.

FIFTY   That is true. You give me courage. I can talk to you. If I
hadn't talked to you I should never have been able to
begin.

FRIEND   But that's all over now.

FIFTY   Do you think so? If you can explain to me what happened,
then it's over – I don't know whether you can. But I'm glad
you were there because now you can answer me precisely.
I mistrust things that I experience alone, because now they
no longer concern me alone. Will you help me?

FRIEND   I will always help you. I can't do otherwise. Ask what you
want. I won't lie any more. I can't lie to you.

FIFTY   Nor can I lie to you when we are talking to each other. But now tell me: how is that I am still alive?

FRIEND   I don't understand. Your moment had not come.

FIFTY   But the Keeper explained to everyone that my moment had come. You were there. You heard him.

FRIEND   He could be wrong for once.

FIFTY   He explained that he was certain of it and I disputed it. He maintained that he knew better and that my mother had misled me. How does he know that? How can he know it?

FRIEND   He has an eye for people. Don't forget that he has immense experience. He was convinced of what he said. Had he not been convinced of it, he would not have brought you before the people.

FIFTY   But why did he?

FRIEND   He wanted to prove to everyone how ridiculous your doubts were. You stood there and with unparalleled obstinacy continued to affirm that you didn't believe it. You would outlive your moment. People had only to leave you alone and you would show them how to do it. They could regard you as an experiment. You didn't believe in the thing and therefore it wouldn't happen to you.

FIFTY   That's correct. That's what I said.

FRIEND   And he knew that it was impossible. He knew that, of yourself, you would fall at the *moment* and he wanted that to happen as publicly as your challenge. You yourself should refute yourself. You may think that unkind and certainly it does seem malicious to make the frailty of man a public entertainment. But don't forget what you had done. You disturbed a funeral and terrified a poor mother who had lost her child. The outcry against you was general and it is the Keeper's duty to safeguard the security of the people. He has to guard against the resurgence of the old fear. Everything depends on the Law of the moment. If he allowed anyone to question that Law, everything would totter. The consequences would be unthinkable. One man

69

would fall on another and we would be back again in the
den of murderers. Are you not glad yourself that it turned
out as it did? He got you to recant and you are alive. What
more do you want?

FIFTY   But I still haven't understood. You haven't answered my
question.

FRIEND   I think it would be better if I asked *you* something. It was
your attitude which no one understood, not the Keeper's.

FIFTY   Ask then, ask.

FRIEND   When you were led forward and the people began to
collect round you, you were silent at first for a long time.
More and more people came, till the square outside was
black with people. Meanwhile you let the whole trial go on
quietly around you without once opening your mouth. To
the Keeper's accusations you just nodded indifferently.
Suddenly, when the judgement had already been given,
you shouted: "It is not my moment!" It sounded immensely
certain and I can tell you that those first words made a
profound impression on the people. The Keeper, however,
seemed to know better and he pressed you hard. You
invoked your memory and your mother. You were quite
certain that it was not your moment. The Keeper repeated
the sentence. I admired you and, in spite of my
unspeakable fear for you, I prayed that you should stand
firm. Then suddenly you began to beg for a day's
postponement and, in exchange for this day, you offered a
confession. The confession was – I still can't understand it –
that it was your moment, exactly the opposite of your first
clear, strong words. – The effect of this contradiction was
terrible. Feeling swung against you immediately. You must
know that since then, everyone without exception has
thought you a charlatan. Can you explain this
contradiction?

FIFTY   Nothing is easier. There is no contradiction. I simply don't
know. I don't know how old I am. I've never bothered about
it. Till a short time ago I never even knew that one should
know such a thing. I really do not know my birthday.

Everyone always made such a secret about theirs. I am a victim of this secret-mongering. So much so that I never even noticed that something always was kept secret. Certainly I must often have been told as a child, but I soon stopped listening. If I ever knew I forgot it later. I have neither squandered my years nor husbanded them. I have never regarded them as capital. I have never thought of years. I have enjoyed living too much to think about years.

FRIEND   You really don't know how old you are?

FIFTY   No. What I said was untrue both times. Both times I lied.

FRIEND   But what sense was there in that?

FIFTY   I wanted to confuse the Keeper. If I deny that it is my moment, how *can* the Keeper prove it? That's what I said to myself. I wanted to confuse him in front of the whole huge crowd of people. I wanted to shake their false belief. Someone must. I am the right man to do it because I do not know my age.

FRIEND   A desperate undertaking. Their belief is not false.

FIFTY   But I've succeeded. Don't you see that I've succeeded?

FRIEND   You shouldn't speak like that. Don't forget that you've recanted.

FIFTY   First I forced him to commit himself. He declared that my moment had come. He was quite certain and everyone heard him. Then I recanted and obtained mercy by it. I am still alive. Either he made a mistake and knows no more about my moment than I do, or it is possible *to outlive the moment itself.* Everyone must now believe one of those two things.

FRIEND   But you're wrong! No one could forget your recantation. It made too deep an impression. To me, what remains of the scene is simply that you contradicted yourself.

FIFTY   That may be. I don't mind. For myself, I am now further on than I ever was. I know now that, sometime at least, the Keeper *lies.* His judgements are uncertain. He himself is uncertain. He contradicts himself and forgives someone who recants. He *needs* the recantation. He would do anything to get a recantation. He is as dependent on it as we, on our side, on a locket.

FRIEND   That was my own impression. I won't hide it from you.

FIFTY   You admit it, you admit it? That was your own impression and you were down below and not in danger and the excitement couldn't deceive you.

FRIEND   Don't think that I was less excited than you were. But I had hoped that your recantation held, that it was final, that you'd had enough of running against the Laws of Nature.

FIFTY   The Laws of Nature? What's that? The rules and regulations of the Keeper? So far I don't even know what a locket looks like inside. If I could increase by ten the years which are written in the locket as prescribed to a man, if I could open it and arbitrarily increase that count by ten – what do you think would happen then?

FRIEND   You would not sin. You would be no man's murderer. I know you too well. You are no murderer. No murderer feels like that. No murderer speaks like that. You will calm down. You've been through great excitement. You will calm down and forget all this and let it rest at the recantation. Promise me.

FIFTY   I promise nothing.

FIFTY   Hi, listen to me! I want to speak to you. What are you running away for? I shan't do anything. Hi, don't run away. I must speak to you.

FIRST OLD WOMAN   (*Out of breath*) We've got nothing.

SECOND OLD WOMAN   Nothing at all.

FIFTY   But I don't want anything. I don't want to take anything from you. I only want to ask you something.

FIRST OLD WOMAN   I'm a stranger here.

SECOND OLD WOMAN   I come from a long way off.

FIFTY   I don't want you to tell me the way. I know the way myself.

FIRST OLD WOMAN   What do you want then?

SECOND OLD WOMAN   We've got nothing and we're strangers here.

FIFTY   You don't need to be frightened of me. Don't you understand that I shan't hurt you? I promise you faithfully, I only want to ask you something. About the old times.

FIRST OLD WOMAN   Very old. But she's older than me.

SECOND OLD WOMAN   She's older. Ask her.

FIFTY   I want to ask you both.

FIRST OLD WOMAN   It's getting late.

SECOND OLD WOMAN   I've got to hurry.

FIFTY   You can't hurry. Afterwards I will take you home as quickly as you want. Just stand still a minute now and listen to what I ask you.

FIRST OLD WOMAN   I'm listening. But I don't know anything.

SECOND OLD WOMAN   I can hear all right. I'm not so old as that. But I don't know what I've got to say.

FIFTY   Listen to me carefully. I want each of you to tell me something. (*To first old woman*). How old are you?

FIRST OLD WOMAN   I'm not old at all.

FIFTY   I know. But *how* old are you?

FIRST OLD WOMAN   I don't know any more. Ask her.

FIFTY   Think about it while I ask her (*to the second*). How old are you?

SECOND OLD WOMAN   I'm not old.

FIFTY   No, but *how old*?

SECOND OLD WOMAN   I've forgotten. Ask her.

FIFTY   (*to the first*). Do you know now? Can you remember?

FIRST OLD WOMAN   No, I don't know. It's too long ago.

FIFTY   If I hit you, will you still not tell me?

FIRST OLD WOMAN   (*Screams*) Help, help! He's going to hit me!

FIFTY   Be quiet. I shan't hit you. What's your name.

FIRST OLD WOMAN   Ninety-Three, but don't hit me. I'll tell you. Ninety-Three.

SECOND OLD WOMAN   I'll tell you too. You can't touch me. My name's Ninety-Six.

FIFTY   You told me before I asked you. You're in a great hurry. How long have you been friends?

BOTH   Ever so long.

FIFTY   But I want to know how long.

FIRST OLD WOMAN   I knew her before I was married.

SECOND OLD WOMAN   And I knew her too.

FIFTY   You were very young, weren't you, when you married?

FIRST OLD WOMAN   Much too young. But nobody knew how young I was then. It was a great secret. It doesn't matter any more now. Everybody's dead now. She's the only one alive now.

SECOND OLD WOMAN   I was always older than her. She always
        came after me.

FIFTY   Now I shall soon know how old you are.

BOTH   Oh no. Nobody knows that.

FIFTY   I only need to look in your lockets.

BOTH   (*Beginning to scream*) That's not true. He's a liar. He's
        lying, he's lying!

FIFTY   Stop that noise. At once.

BOTH   (*Shrieking louder all the time*) It's not true. Nobody knows
        that. He's lying, he's lying!

FIFTY   I shall hit you both. If you don't stop screaming at once, I
        shall hit you.

FIRST OLD WOMAN   (*Trembling*) I've stopped. I'm so frightened.

SECOND OLD WOMAN   I want to stop. But I can't. I'm afraid.

FIFTY   Give me your lockets. At once.

FIRST OLD WOMAN   I've got no locket.

SECOND OLD WOMAN   I've lost mine. (*They are both quite calm
        now*).

FIFTY   I shall find them. You've both got them still. Give them to
        me. I need them.

FIRST OLD WOMAN   I've eaten mine.

FIFTY   (*Patting her back*) Then spit it out.

FIRST OLD WOMAN   (*Spitting and spitting*) It won't come.

FIFTY   Never mind. Better give it to me at once. Or I'll kill you.

SECOND OLD WOMAN   (*Trembling*) I've found mine. Here it is
        (*she hands the locket to him*) She's got hers too. Just look
        for it.

FIRST OLD WOMAN   You should be ashamed. You only want
        me to lose mine too.

FIFTY   Give it with a good grace. You see, she's given me hers.

FIRST OLD WOMAN   (*Hands him her locket, weeping*) What shall I do without my locket?

SECOND OLD WOMAN   What will happen to us now?

FIFTY   I'll give you another in exchange, prettier, made of gold.

BOTH   Made of gold. Made of gold.

FIFTY   (*Hangs a locket round the neck of each*) There. Now you've got much nicer ones. Now you're satisfied, aren't you? Now you'll live much, much longer. These are lucky lockets. I make them myself. But you must say nothing to anyone. If you say nothing to anyone, you'll both live longer. You want to do that, don't you? Don't you?

FIRST OLD WOMAN   Oh, yes! Much longer.

SECOND OLD WOMAN   Much, much longer.

FIFTY   When I see you next time, I'll give you still better ones. I shall find you. I know where you live. Now you must go away quite quietly. You must promise me that you'll say nothing to anyone. Otherwise everyone will want pretty gold lockets and I only have these two. If people know they'll want to take them away from you. Will you hold your tongues?

FIRST OLD WOMAN   Oh yes, yes!

SECOND OLD WOMAN   But I'll get a better one.

FIFTY   You shall have a better one. But I shall have to look for it. That's not so easy. I must go away now. When I come back and see you again, then you shall have the other lockets. You've got time now. But go away quickly before anyone notices. They'll take them from you if you don't look out.

BOTH   (*Hobbling quickly away*) Thank you, Sir, thank you.

76

FIFTY. THE FRIEND.

FIFTY   I've got two lockets.

FRIEND   What have you got?

FIFTY   I've got two lockets. Two real lockets.

FRIEND   In God's name, where did you get them?

FIFTY   I've got them from two old women. They belong to me
now. I can do what I want with them.

FRIEND   I . . . I won't look at them.

FIFTY   That doesn't alter the fact that I have them.

FRIEND   This is terrible. Give them back at once.

FIFTY   I gave them better ones.

FRIEND   Better?

FIFTY   Yes, better. Made of gold.

FRIEND   But those are false.

FIFTY   No, they are better. They run for longer.

FRIEND   Where did you get them from?

FIFTY   That I shan't say. I had them and I gave them to two old
women who gave me theirs in exchange.

FRIEND   They must have been half-witted. No one would do that
willingly.

FIFTY   I helped them a little.

FRIEND   You mean, you took them by force. Do you know what
you are?

FIFTY   It doesn't interest me what I am. Everyone is something. So
I am something too. But I have two lockets and I can do
what I want with them.

FRIEND   Go away. Why do you tell me all this?

FIFTY   You can denounce me. If you are afraid, I will release you from our friendship. I shan't be angry with you. You're trembling.

FRIEND   Why, what should I be afraid of? I have done nothing. I feel guilty. If only I had never spoken to you. I started you along this path. I should never have answered your question. I am to blame for everything. I am the criminal. And should I then betray you?

FIFTY   Don't worry about that. Help me, rather, help me. It's done now.

FRIEND   How should I help you? You know what you are now.

FIFTY   A murderer. A common murderer, or whatever it's called. Help me to open the lockets.

FRIEND   Open them? You want to open them?

FIFTY   I want to see what's inside them. You know what should be inside.

FRIEND   But what sense is there in that if you know what you'll find?

FIFTY   Do I know?

FRIEND   Yes, of course. Every child knows. After all, everyone wears them their whole life long. Everyone knows.

FIFTY   Have you ever seen inside one?

FRIEND   No. But one doesn't need to.

FIFTY   You've never seen one?

FRIEND   But I was there when they prepared my father's body for burial. I was there when – must I say it all again? You know how her death still hurts me. I was there. Do you understand? I was there. I was there when the examiner found the locket and opened it. I was there when he made the entry.

FIFTY   Did you see inside?

FRIEND   No. You ask for too much. I was too upset. Should I have noticed figures then? But a lot of other people were there. Do you imagine there were no witnesses?

FIFTY   They were as much upset as you were. *No one* saw inside the lockets. No one. The only person who was not upset was the Keeper himself. He is never upset. He sees them all and registers them all.

FRIEND   And you don't believe him because you hate him. I should never have sent you to him.

FIFTY   Listen to me. I hate no one. But I believe no one. It is too important to me. I want to open the lockets myself and look at them myself. I *will* open them. You must accept that. No one will stop me doing it. I want you to help me.

FRIEND   I will help you. But how can I? What can I do to help? It's half done already.

FIFTY   I need your eyes. I want you to look inside the lockets with me. I don't trust my eyes. I am prejudiced. If I tell you what I see you won't believe me.

FRIEND   Now I understand. You want me to be there when you open them?

FIFTY   Exactly. Don't desert me now. You *understand* what it's about.

FRIEND   I don't understand what it's about. Perhaps I don't want to understand.

FIFTY   But you won't desert me?

FRIEND   No. I won't desert you.

FIFTY   Here they are. How can we open them?

FRIEND   It will be very difficult. The Keeper has a key.

FIFTY   We shall have to break them open.

FRIEND   I am afraid so. There's no other way.

FIFTY   Have you a hammer?

FRIEND   Here.

FIFTY   Thank you. Now.

FRIEND   Carefully, carefully. You don't want to crush what's inside.

FIFTY   (*Hits it*) There.

FRIEND   Show me. Is it open?

FIFTY   No, only bent. They're strangely made.

FRIEND   What do we do now?

FIFTY   I shall hammer it again. (*Hammers*). Now give me a file.

FRIEND   Here.

FIFTY   I think this will do it. Wait. Can you hold it?

FRIEND   There. I've got the chain firm.

FIFTY   It's open! It's open! Look carefully inside. You look first. What do you see?

FRIEND   Nothing.

FIFTY   Nothing. It's empty.

FRIEND   Empty. It's a mistake. Where's the other one?

FIFTY   Here. Give me the hammer. (*He hammers it*). The file. Hold it. Now. (*He files*). It's open. This time I'll look first.

FRIEND   No, together.

FIFTY   Better alone. Let me first.

FRIEND   As you like. What do you see?

FIFTY   Nothing. Nothing. It's empty.

FRIEND   What? That one too? – Yes, it's empty. What does it mean?

FIFTY   That's what I ask you.

FRIEND   The old women cheated you. They didn't give you the real lockets.

FIFTY   Do you think so? I don't. You weren't there. You would have had to be there.

FRIEND   But you can see that they're empty.

FIFTY   Lockets *are* empty. Don't you understand that?

FRIEND   They can't be. You're mad.

FIFTY   Here's mine. Give me yours. We'll open them both.

FRIEND   I – I can't. Forgive me. I can't give you mine and I don't
want you to open yours either.

FIFTY   You can't stop me. I don't need yours. Here's mine.
Hammer it.

FRIEND   No.

FIFTY   Coward. Give me the hammer.

FRIEND   I . . . I can't give it to you.

FIFTY   Then I shall take it. I am not afraid.

FRIEND   What are you doing? What are you doing?

FIFTY   You are like the old women. (*He hammers*). Now I've
crushed it. Help me with the file.

FRIEND   I'm holding it.

FIFTY   Open! Open! My own locket is open. Look inside it. I
appoint you my Keeper. What do you see?

FRIEND   (*Trembling*). Nothing. It's empty.

FIFTY   Nothing. Empty too. *All lockets are empty.*

FRIEND   It's not possible. Go away, go. You've played a wicked
trick on me. You're no longer my friend. What do you
mean with this farce, with false lockets that you pretend to
have stolen, false lockets that you hang round yourself?
You find it amusing, but to me it's nothing but bitterness. I'll
never see you again. Do you think you can give me back
my sister with these cruel jokes? Go away. I hate you. I hate
you.

FIFTY   You don't believe me? Well, give me your own locket
before you condemn me. Can I have put that round your
neck? You know your own locket. You condemn me. You

81

are not only my best friend. You are my only friend. You attribute such meanness to me. Give me the chance of defending myself. Sacrifice your locket to me. Here you stand. You have it on you. You've always had it on you. Never once in your life have you taken it off. Not once. I'll go into the furthest corner of the room. I'll stay there. I won't move. Open your own locket. You owe that to me. Do it. Do it.

FRIEND   I can't. I am afraid of you. What do you want with me? Leave me in peace.

FIFTY   You don't want to know me any more?

FRIEND   I want you to leave me in peace.

FIFTY   I'm going. Goodbye.

FRIEND   You're going. But how shall I live now?

FIFTY   I have done nothing to you.

FRIEND   Nothing. Nothing. Then go. Go. Go.

FIFTY   I bear you no ill-will. Goodbye.

FRIEND   No. You bear me no ill-will. But I bear ill-will towards you. I hate you. Go.

FIFTY   What should I do?

FRIEND   Nothing. But go.

FIFTY   Very well. Goodbye.

FIFTY   And all those who have died too soon?

KEEPER   No one has died too soon.

FIFTY   My friend had a sister who died when she was twelve.

KEEPER   That was her lawful name.

FIFTY   Lawful! A law that is built on ignorance!

KEEPER   There are no other laws. With laws only one thing matters: that they should be observed.

FIFTY   By everyone?

KEEPER   By everyone who lives within their jurisdiction.

FIFTY   And someone who lived before?

KEEPER   He could not observe it. Have you another urgent and intelligent question?

FIFTY   What would happen if men suddenly learned that all lockets were empty?

KEEPER   They could not learn that. Who would tell them something so stupid? Who would tell them something so terrible?

FIFTY   Let us suppose that someone had the delusion that all lockets were empty and went like a town crier through the streets, or like a new Mohammed. Instead of "God is great and Mohammed is his prophet" he would cry "The lockets are empty and no one knows it! The lockets are empty and no one knows it!"

KEEPER   No one would believe him. He would soon be silent.

FIFTY   And if he emptied a locket and with the empty husk ran through the streets?

KEEPER   It is no secret what happens to murderers.

FIFTY   But I am anxious. I am terribly anxious. Once spoken aloud, the thought would spread and strike roots.

KEEPER   Your anxiety is a credit to you and should be remembered in your favour. But generations of Keepers have thought about it and guarded against it. Not for nothing is the stigma of murderer laid upon locket thieves. You see that it has worked so far.

FIFTY   But I am thinking about the future.

KEEPER   You think too much about the future. A remnant of your rebellious period.

FIFTY   Does this remnant seem to you disquieting? Do you consider my excess of zeal harmful?

KEEPER   I won't say that. You can be dangerous no longer. You have publicly recanted. You are considered a coward and a fool. Even if you returned to your vociferous doubts, you could no longer make any impression with them. Only the innocent are really believed. An apostate is wholly identified with his new faith and the old is lost to him more entirely than ever he intended himself.

FIFTY   Why do you think I could lapse again?

KEEPER   I don't think so. I have only explained to you why you can no longer be dangerous. Whatever you did would be fruitless.

FIFTY   But do you disapprove of my anxieties?

KEEPER   There is harmless knowledge and there is dangerous knowledge. But there are doubts which are more dangerous still. From these you have been saved for always.

FIFTY   What do you mean by that?

KEEPER   Nothing definite. There are doubts which make men mad. Even dangerous knowledge is better than those. A man can keep that to himself.

FIFTY   I have frightened you. I should not have said that the lockets could be empty.

KEEPER   You have not frightened me in the least. You opened your locket and found nothing in it. I have done that a thousand times. Do I look frightened?

FIFTY   Do you really believe that I could have done such a thing?

KEEPER   There is no need for belief. No one who has not opened
a locket ever conceived such a suspicion as yours. You are
a murderer. But we are not interested in murderers who
recant in time.

FIFTY   You accuse me of murder without any proof.

KEEPER   I dispense with proof. It would be too easy. You have
your freedom. You know too that you will live as long –
now – as you in fact live. This was the freedom you were
concerned with. You have stolen it for yourself. Enjoy it to
your heart's content. Be assured that there are other fools
like you who prefer this deadly uncertainty to the calm
which we established and which we maintain.

FIFTY   Are there really others?

KEEPER   Be assured that you are not unique. You discovered that
you were nothing out of the ordinary when, for the sake of
one day of life, you were ready to recant. You were so
cowardly that you cannot even admit your cowardice. But
now you will be able to enjoy your cowardice to the full.
For, instead of *one moment*, you have before you nothing
but such moments. I do not intend to let you be arrested as
a murderer. Rejoice in your gain. I leave you your fear.

*FIFTY IN THE STREET. LIKE A TOWN CRIER. BUT ALSO LIKE
ONE POSSESSED.*

FIFTY   I will not know you. You are nothing to me. You are
nothing to me for you are not here. You are not alive. You
are all dead, I am the only one. I am alive. I do not know
when I shall die. Therefore I am the only one.
You creep about with that precious little load around your
necks. Your years hang round your necks. Are they heavy
to carry? No, they are not heavy for they are not many. But
you do not mind. For you are dead already. I do not see
you at all. You are not even shadows. You are nothing. I

85

come among you only that you may feel how I despise you.
Listen, you people, you fine dead, the years that you carry
around your necks are false. You think you have them.
You are so certain. But nothing is certain. It is all false. You
have empty lockets hanging round your necks. The lockets
are empty. You have not even the years that you think you
have. You have nothing. Nothing is certain. The lockets are
empty. Everything is as uncertain as it ever was. He who
desires to die, can die today. He who does not desire it,
dies nonetheless. The lockets are empty. The lockets are
empty.

THE YOUNG MEN

FIRST YOUNG MAN   Here comes the Deliverer.

SECOND YOUNG MAN   The Deliverer! The Deliverer!

FIRST YOUNG MAN   What did he actually do?

SECOND YOUNG MAN   He looked inside the locket.

FIRST YOUNG MAN   I could have done that too.

SECOND YOUNG MAN   Why didn't you try it?

FIRST YOUNG MAN   I didn't think of it.

SECOND YOUNG MAN   That's the point. It's not as easy as you
    think.

FIRST YOUNG MAN   Have you tried?

SECOND YOUNG MAN   To be honest, yes. One can't open the
    thing.

FIRST YOUNG MAN   What did you do with it then?

SECOND YOUNG MAN   I just threw it away.

FIRST YOUNG MAN   I couldn't. No. Not that.

SECOND YOUNG MAN   Do you think yours is something special?

FIRST YOUNG MAN   Things can change.

SECOND YOUNG MAN   What can change?

FIRST YOUNG MAN   I shall wait until the Keeper has spoken.

SECOND YOUNG MAN   The Keeper! The swindler.

FIRST YOUNG MAN   You're a bit rash.

SECOND YOUNG MAN   Blockhead. You can't live without some kind of swindle.

FIRST YOUNG MAN   Honestly. I don't like the change.

SECOND YOUNG MAN   Why? Why?

FIRST YOUNG MAN   Have you really considered it?

SECOND YOUNG MAN   There's not all that to consider. The lockets are empty.

FIRST YOUNG MAN   Have you examined *all* lockets?

SECOND YOUNG MAN   What are you implying?

FIRST YOUNG MAN   Perhaps some are empty, and perhaps in some there is something.

SECOND YOUNG MAN   You're hopeless. That would be more of a swindle still.

FIRST YOUNG MAN   It's easy enough to talk. But what will happen to us all now?

SECOND YOUNG MAN   What will happen? What will happen. We are free now.

FIRST YOUNG MAN   In what way?

SECOND YOUNG MAN   I am no longer afraid that I shall have to die when I am twenty-eight.

FIRST YOUNG MAN   And I am afraid that I shall die before I am eighty–eight.

SECOND YOUNG MAN   You have been favoured till now. People like you will be done away with.

FIRST YOUNG MAN   But why? Why? What have I done to you?

SECOND YOUNG MAN   What have you done to me? You were a God. All on account of your damned name. Why should you be called Eighty-Eight and I Twenty-Eight? Are you better than I am? Are you cleverer or more hardworking? On the contrary: you are stupider, nastier and lazier. But it was always Eighty-Eight this – Eighty-Eight that.

FIRST YOUNG MAN   I never noticed it.

SECOND YOUNG MAN   And you never noticed either that all the girls ran after you. Whenever you appeared, it was an occasion. You could have married the lot. But you didn't have to marry anyone. It was an honour even to breathe the odour of your splendid name.

FIRST YOUNG MAN   But that was always a burden to me. You have no idea how burdensome it all was.

SECOND YOUNG MAN   It wasn't noticeable. You put up with it quite calmly.

FIRST YOUNG MAN   What should I have done?

SECOND YOUNG MAN   You got the most benefit out of this swindle. Did it ever *once* occur to you to look inside your locket?

FIRST YOUNG MAN   No, it didn't occur to me. And you? Why did you never look?

SECOND YOUNG MAN   Because I was afraid. No one likes to label himself a murderer.

FIRST YOUNG MAN   It was a good law. Everything was peaceful.

SECOND YOUNG MAN   And now you're not peaceful?

FIRST YOUNG MAN   No one is. No one. Not only I. Do you know that you won't fall down dead in the next hour?

SECOND YOUNG MAN   No. I don't know. But it's better, it's
        more *just* than it was, for I know that you too, in the next
        moment, may fall down dead.

FIRST YOUNG MAN   And that's to your advantage?

SECOND YOUNG MAN   It's everything.

FIRST YOUNG MAN   You're eaten up with envy. I don't know
        what envy is.

SECOND YOUNG MAN   You'll soon get accustomed to envy. Be
        patient for a little.

FIRST YOUNG MAN   What will happen to our Keeper?

SECOND YOUNG MAN   He will be tried.

FIRST YOUNG MAN   One can't do that. One can't condemn him
        for abiding by his oath of office. He will be acquitted.

SECOND YOUNG MAN   He certainly will not. You'll see your
        marvels yet. If the Keeper is acquitted, there will be a
        revolution.

FIRST YOUNG MAN   There you're wrong. The Deliverer himself
        wants everything to pass off without bloodshed.

SECOND YOUNG MAN   Deliverer. What that sounds like on your
        lips! You *hate* him really. Better watch what you say about
        him.

FIRST YOUNG MAN   I've said nothing against him.

SECOND YOUNG MAN   But I can feel it behind your words. The
        hatred is unmistakable.

FIRST YOUNG MAN   Oh, you know best about everything.

SECOND YOUNG MAN   No, but I've had enough of your calling
        the tune. I've had enough, enough, enough.

FIRST YOUNG MAN   Who would have thought that you are my
        brother?

SECOND YOUNG MAN   Yes, who would have thought it when
        you were called Eighty-Eight and I Twenty-Eight?

THE TWO COLLEAGUES

FIRST COLLEAGUE   It seems that people were not all so contented.

SECOND COLLEAGUE   Much hate has gathered.

FIRST COLLEAGUE   Who would have thought it? The people are frenzied. I have just lived through a scene that I shall never forget.

SECOND COLLEAGUE   What was that?

FIRST COLLEAGUE   A sea of people, the street black with people, and suddenly a man was heaved up on their shoulders who cried out loud, "Away with lockets! Who needs that rubbish? Away with lockets!" He ripped open his shirt and tore out the locket and hurled it down among the people. The people shouted for joy. Some copied him, first men, then women too. They clawed their breasts and tore out the lockets. "Away with lockets!" Then another leapt up and roared, "Now there will be no more dying. Now everyone will live as long as he wants. Freedom! Freedom!" And "Freedom! Freedom! as long as we want!" roared back the crowd. I felt it myself. I did like the others. I felt as if someone urged my hand to my breast. I tore the thing out and flung it away. "No more lockets! No more lockets! No more dying!" And the frenzied crowd took up my cry and everyone shouted "No more dying! No more dying!"

SECOND COLLEAGUE   But what does that mean? It means nothing.

FIRST COLLEAGUE   It means what it means. They have had enough of dying. Haven't you had enough?

SECOND COLLEAGUE   Yes.

FIRST COLLEAGUE   What do you want then? What are you bleating for? What do you object to? Men have discovered their right to live.

SECOND COLLEAGUE   And will everyone now decide how long he wants to live?

FIRST COLLEAGUE   There is not much to decide. Everyone will
    live for ever.

SECOND COLLEAGUE   Everyone will live for ever. That sounds
    wonderful.

FIRST COLLEAGUE   It doesn't sound wonderful. It is wonderful.

SECOND COLLEAGUE   But is it also true?

FIRST COLLEAGUE   You are the eternal doubter. I bet you still
    have your locket. You like to be careful, don't you? You like
    to keep what you have. You don't like risking anything.
    You're a hero. Have you got it or have you not?

SECOND COLLEAGUE   What does it matter to you?

FIRST COLLEAGUE   It matters very much to me.

SECOND COLLEAGUE   I can do what I like with my locket.

FIRST COLLEAGUE   That's what you think. Give it to me. At
    once. It must be destroyed.

SECOND COLLEAGUE   No, I shall not give it to you. I shall keep
    my locket.

FIRST COLLEAGUE   You will not keep it. Give it to me. At once.
    (*He starts to choke him*)

SECOND COLLEAGUE   Help! He's killing me! He's taking my
    locket. Murder! Murder!

FIRST COLLEAGUE   That's no longer murder, fool. Give me
    your locket or there will be murder.

SECOND COLLEAGUE   (*Trembling*) Take it. I won't stop you,
    but you'll regret it.

FIRST COLLEAGUE   Regret it? Fool! When? Why? There's the
    empty cheating thing. Tread on it!

SECOND COLLEAGUE   I can't!

FIRST COLLEAGUE   Trample on it, or I'll kill you.

SECOND COLLEAGUE   (*Treads on it, his whole body quivering,
    and falls down dead*)

FIFTY   But where will it end?

KEEPER   There will be no end. Everything is crumbling.

FIFTY   I should not have begun.

KEEPER   It is too late now.

FIFTY   The mischief is done. Can I save nothing?

KEEPER   Every murderer has asked that, but only when everything is irrevocable.

FIFTY   And if I set an example? If I went before the people again and boldly and honestly admitted my crime, really honestly this time? If I warned them and then, to prove my warning, fell down dead before them? Is there nothing I can do now that will make any impression?
Nothing I can do which will help them? There may be others later who do as I did and suffer shipwreck and bring confusion into the world. I am so much ashamed. Most of all I am ashamed of my blindness.

KEEPER   It is too late. It is too late. I fear that you have achieved your purpose.

FIFTY   You mean that everyone knows now?

KEEPER   You chose your night-watchman's cry too well. I would not have believed that you would be heard so soon and so clearly.

FIFTY   You underestimated me. You are to blame.

KEEPER   Do you really think that? Do you believe it?

FIFTY   *You* were set as watchman. You held a high and noble office. You knew, too, *what* you watched. You came against me with pride and power. You should have destroyed me at once. How could you underrate me so? Where was your experience?

KEEPER   My experience is of the dead.

FIFTY You were intent on your dead and on the pomp and vanity
       of your office. Did you have no opportunity to observe the
       living, the relatives of your dead? Did all your solemnities
       run their preordained and formal course? Did nothing
       happen, ever? Did nothing unexpected happen, ever?

KEEPER No, nothing happened, ever.

FIFTY What kind of men did you live among?

KEEPER Among contented men. Among men who were no
        longer afraid.

FIFTY Then there was indeed little more to learn.

FIFTY AND HIS FRIEND MEET AGAIN.

FRIEND Is that you?

FIFTY Yes. Don't you know me?

FRIEND I don't know anything for certain now.

FIFTY What's the matter? What's happened to you?

FRIEND I am looking for my sister.

FIFTY But you can't be looking for her.

FRIEND She's hiding.

FIFTY Hiding? What do you mean?

FRIEND She's hiding and I don't know where. I am looking
        everywhere.

FIFTY But are you sure?

FRIEND   I know she is. I know it.

FIFTY   But why should she be hiding from you?

FRIEND   She was afraid.

FIFTY   Of what?

FRIEND   She was afraid of her name. People told her she had to
die when she was twelve. They were after her. For years she
was afraid. She grew quieter and quieter. We didn't know
why she spoke so little. We had no idea. But then, on her
birthday, fear seized her. She disappeared. She went away
among people who did not know her name. She was afraid
of her name. Since then she has been hiding. No one of us
has seen her again. She has avoided us like the plague. But
we are looking for her everywhere. At least, it is I who am
really looking for her. I do nothing else any more now. I
know I shall find her.

FIFTY   But why do you want to disturb her? Let her lead her new
life. It will be better for her if she is not disturbed. Her fear
must have been very great or she would not have hidden
herself for so long. If I am not mistaken, it's more than thirty
years ago now.

FRIEND   Yes, it is. That's why it's so hard to find her. Often I think
I wouldn't recognize her any more. But I only think that
when I'm tired and weak from searching and almost lose
heart. But when I feel like that, I go and have a long sleep
and then, as soon as I'm fresh and rested, I don't doubt any
more that I shall recognize her, at once, even from far off,
even, if it has to be in thirty years from now. She has only to
come towards me and I shall take her gently by the hand,
quite gently, as if I wanted to stroke her, but not like a
strange man, like this – you see – and then I shall tell her
that it's me.

FIFTY   She will think you want to arrest her.

FRIEND   (*Angry*) I arrest her? My little sister? How can you say
that? You're out of your mind.

FIFTY   Please understand me. Of course you don't want to arrest her. You want to do for her what is best and most loving. But, if she went away in terror of her name, she will believe that she did something wrong. She avoids you so as not to be punished for that wrong.

FRIEND   She did no wrong. She was frightened and with reason. She was a child, terrified by silly talk.

FIFTY   That's what I mean. She has made a new life for herself. She keeps away from you because she doesn't want to be dragged back to the old life. Only among new faces does she feel safe and unrecognized.

FRIEND   I will tell her the truth. I will tell her that her name means nothing. I will take away her fear. Then she will come back to us.

FIFTY   But don't you see that she will have a new name now? She must have taken a new name, otherwise her flight would have had no sense.

FRIEND   She will tell me about it. She will tell me what her name is now.

FIFTY   And what will you call her?

FRIEND   To me she is my little sister. She has not changed. She is what she always was. My dearest little sister. The dearest thing in the world.

FIFTY   But thirty years older.

FRIEND   How stupid of you to think that. She has not aged at all.

FIFTY   I don't say that she has aged, but that she is thirty years older and must have changed.

FRIEND   I don't think so.

FIFTY   You mustn't be obstinate. She is now forty-two. She can't look like a child of twelve.

FRIEND   To me she is twelve.

FIFTY   And will you still call her by that name?

FRIEND   Of course. What should I call her? Twelve, Twelve, I shall say and I shall take her in my arms and pull her hair as I always used to and toss her and swing her and hold her out of the window till she screams for mercy. Twelve, Twelve, I shall say, don't you see that it's all nonsense? All names are nonsense. It doesn't matter what one's name is. Twelve or Eighty-Eight, or the devil knows what, if we are here together and see each other and speak to each other. Twelve, do you hear me? Twelve, do you see me? Twelve, it's me. Twelve, it will always be me.

FIFTY   But she? How do you know that she will be as pleased about it as you are? Perhaps she's much happier now. Perhaps she didn't like living among you. Perhaps she always longed to leave you.

FRIEND   Perhaps, perhaps, perhaps! I know what I'm talking about. For me there is no perhaps.

FIFTY   Why don't you let her live as *she wants to live?* You want to force her to come back to you. That's not right. That's not fair. You don't really love her. If you did, you would feel bound to let her live as *she* wants to. Unless you're just talking, you must renounce her.

FRIEND   I'm not just talking. That's why I'm looking for her. That's why I shall find her.